MW01025929

GRUESOME PLAYGROUND INJURIES

BY RAJIV JOSEPH

★

★

DRAMATISTS
PLAY SERVICE
INC.

GRUESOME PLAYGROUND INJURIES
Copyright © 2012, Rajiv Joseph

All Rights Reserved

CAUTION: Professionals and amateurs are hereby warned that performance of GRUESOME PLAYGROUND INJURIES is subject to payment of a royalty. It is fully protected under the copyright laws of the United States of America, and of all countries covered by the International Copyright Union (including the Dominion of Canada and the rest of the British Commonwealth), and of all countries covered by the Pan-American Copyright Convention, the Universal Copyright Convention, the Berne Convention, and of all countries with which the United States has reciprocal copyright relations. All rights, including without limitation professional/amateur stage rights, motion picture, recitation, lecturing, public reading, radio broadcasting, television, video or sound recording, all other forms of mechanical, electronic and digital reproduction, transmission and distribution, such as CD, DVD, the Internet, private and file-sharing networks, information storage and retrieval systems, photocopying, and the rights of translation into foreign languages are strictly reserved. Particular emphasis is placed upon the matter of readings, permission for which must be secured from the Author's agent in writing.

The English language stock and amateur stage performance rights in the United States, its territories, possessions and Canada for GRUESOME PLAYGROUND INJURIES are controlled exclusively by DRAMATISTS PLAY SERVICE, INC., 440 Park Avenue South, New York, NY 10016. No professional or nonprofessional performance of the Play may be given without obtaining in advance the written permission of DRAMATISTS PLAY SERVICE, INC., and paying the requisite fee.

Inquiries concerning all other rights should be addressed to the Gersh Agency, 41 Madison Avenue, 33rd Floor, New York, NY 10010. Attn: Seth Glewen.

SPECIAL NOTE

Anyone receiving permission to produce GRUESOME PLAYGROUND INJURIES is required to give credit to the Author as sole and exclusive Author of the Play on the title page of all programs distributed in connection with performances of the Play and in all instances in which the title of the Play appears for purposes of advertising, publicizing or otherwise exploiting the Play and/or a production thereof. The name of the Author must appear on a separate line, in which no other name appears, immediately beneath the title and in size of type equal to 50% of the size of the largest, most prominent letter used for the title of the Play. No person, firm or entity may receive credit larger or more prominent than that accorded the Author. The following acknowledgments must appear on the title page in all programs distributed in connection with performances of the Play:

The World Premiere of GRUESOME PLAYGROUND INJURIES
was produced by the Alley Theatre,
Gregory Boyd, Artistic Director; Dean R. Gladden, Managing Director.

Produced by Second Stage Theatre, New York, January 2011,
Carole Rothman, Artistic Director.

For Keith Benjamin

AUTHOR'S NOTE

All transitions between the scenes should be done by the actors, and their changing of the scene should be leisurely. Costume changes should occur on stage. There is no need to hide any of this work from the audience. We should especially see Doug's dressing of his wounds, or the application of the necessary make-up that represents his injuries. The lengths of the transitions signify and allow for large passages of time in the lives of the characters. Every scene either jumps forward fifteen years or backward ten years.

At times in the dialogue, there are questions but no question mark is written. Absence of a question mark is purposeful. When there is no question mark, the question is delivered in a flat, non-inquiring tone.

I would offer one recommendation to the actor playing the part of Kayleen: Given the emotional stress of the role, the temptation to break down into tears might be very strong. Even so, it is my intention that Kayleen would never allow Doug to see her cry. This is not to say that she cannot come close to tears, but it is a line she will not cross in the presence of another person. The only moments in the play that Kayleen might allow herself to well up would be in Scene 4 (Age Twenty-Eight: Tuesday) and at the very end of the play. But I would ask that even in these moments, a choice to cry is approached with caution.

GRUESOME PLAYGROUND INJURIES received its world premiere at the Alley Theatre (Gregory Boyd, Artistic Director; Dean R. Gladden, Managing Director) in Houston, Texas on October 16, 2009. It was directed by Rebecca Taichman; the set design was by Riccardo Hernandez; the costume design was by Miranda Hoffman; the lighting design was by Christopher Akerlind; the sound design was by Jill BC Du Boff; the dramaturg was Mark Bly; and the stage manager was Elizabeth M. Berther. The cast was as follows:

KAYLEEN ....Selma Blair
DOUG ....Brad Fleischer

GRUESOME PLAYGROUND INJURIES received its New York premiere at Second Stage Theatre (Carole Rothman, Artistic Director; Casey Reitz, Executive Director) on January 31, 2011. It was directed by Scott Ellis; the set design was by Neil Patel; the costume design was by Jeff Mahshie; the lighting design was by Donald Holder; the sound design was by Ryan Rumery; the original music was by Gwendolyn Sanford and Brandon Jay; and the stage manager was Davin DeSantis. The cast was as follows:

KAYLEEN ....Jennifer Carpenter
DOUG ....Pablo Schreiber

CHARACTERS

KAYLEEN, ages 8 – 38

DOUG, ages 8 – 38

PLACE

Various places.

TIME

Over the course of thirty years.

GRUESOME PLAYGROUND INJURIES

Scene 1

Age Eight: Face Split Open

A nurse's office in an elementary school.

Kayleen, 8, lies on a bed, not sleeping. She begins to hit the mattress with her hands rhythmically. She stops. She sits up. She stands on the bed, absently. She's bored. She bounces a little on the bed, and then stops.

A sound of someone coming from outside. Kayleen drops back down and pretends to sleep.

Doug, 8, enters. He has a large gauze bandage wrapped and taped across his face. An awful dark stain of blood grows in the middle of the bandage. He seems dazed, but not hurt, not crying.

He sits on the edge of the other bed and stares at Kayleen. She sits up.

KAYLEEN. What happened to your face?
DOUG. I fell.
KAYLEEN. Why.
DOUG. I don't know.
KAYLEEN. Does it hurt?
DOUG. A little.

KAYLEEN. I have a stomach ache. Sometimes food makes me sick. My mom says it's because I have bad thoughts.

DOUG. Like what?

KAYLEEN. Bad thoughts.

DOUG. Like about Dracula?

KAYLEEN. About stomachs.

DOUG. I have bad thoughts about Dracula.

KAYLEEN. Yeah.

DOUG. Blood tastes funny. It tastes like fruit.

KAYLEEN. It does not.

DOUG. Have you ever cut your face open?

KAYLEEN. No.

DOUG. I get cut all the time by accident.

KAYLEEN. I like the nurse's office. It is quiet and dark.

DOUG. I had a stomach ache when I went and saw the movies.

KAYLEEN. I like the movies except when I come out and there is sun.

DOUG. I had three big Cokes. And I had Gummi Worms. I like to swallow them like real worms.

KAYLEEN. Why do you have so much blood?

DOUG. Because I fell.

KAYLEEN. Why'd you fall?

DOUG. I rode my bike off the roof.

KAYLEEN. What roof?

DOUG. This roof.

KAYLEEN. The school roof?

DOUG. Yeah.

KAYLEEN. Why.

DOUG. I was playing Evel Knievel.

KAYLEEN. What's Evel Knieval?

DOUG. He's a motorcycle guy. That's how I broke my face.

KAYLEEN. Your face isn't broken, it's just cut.

DOUG. Sister Mary Pat said I broke my face.

KAYLEEN. Does it hurt?

DOUG. One time? I went ice skating with my brothers? And I fell on the ice and this girl skated by me and her ice skate cut my eyelid open and I was bleeding out of my eye. I couldn't see because of all the blood.

KAYLEEN. Did it hurt?

DOUG. No, because the eyelid is small even though there is a lot of blood. I have a scar on my eye. Girls don't get scars.

KAYLEEN. Yes we do.

DOUG. How come?

KAYLEEN. If you rode your bike off the roof, then how did you get the bike on the roof?

DOUG. I climbed up a tree.

KAYLEEN. You took your bike with you up the tree?

DOUG. Yeah.

KAYLEEN. Why.

DOUG. So I could ride it off the roof.

KAYLEEN. And then you rode your bike off the roof?

DOUG. Yeah. *(Beat.)*

KAYLEEN. You're stupid.

DOUG. I am not.

KAYLEEN. Yes you are.

DOUG. Shut up.

KAYLEEN. You shut up. *(Long silence.)* One time, I threw up because I had a stomach ache and I threw up so bad that my one eye started to have blood in it.

DOUG. Why.

KAYLEEN. Because I threw up so hard and so there was blood in my eye.

DOUG. Did it hurt?

KAYLEEN. No. But it was red. I have a sensitive stomach. The doctor told me. There's an angel on the roof.

DOUG. No there's not.

KAYLEEN. Yes there is. It's a statue. Are you going to go to the doctors?

DOUG. To get stitches. I like to get stitches.

KAYLEEN. Why.

DOUG. It makes your skin feel tight.

KAYLEEN. Does it hurt?

DOUG. Yeah. *(Kayleen gets up and wanders around the room.)*

KAYLEEN. This room is like a dungeon.

DOUG. What's a dungeon?

KAYLEEN. It's a room in a castle. It's where people languish.

DOUG. Oh.

KAYLEEN. The rest of the castle is loud and has bright lights and flags and hot oil because of wars. But the dungeon is where people can go to languish and get some peace and quiet.

DOUG. *(Sudden; with great pain.)* OW!

KAYLEEN. What?

DOUG. *(Normal.)* My face hurts. I broke it.

KAYLEEN. You did not. It's just cut. Can I see it?

DOUG. What?

KAYLEEN. Can I see the cut on your face?

DOUG. Why.

KAYLEEN. Can I? *(Doug slowly takes off his gauze bandage to reveal a huge gash. Kayleen looks at it for a long time. Doug looks at Kayleen looking at his wounds.)* Does it hurt?

DOUG. A little. *(Kayleen continues looking at his cut, Doug continues looking at her.)* What happened to the blood in your eye?

KAYLEEN. It went back into my head. *(They continue looking at each other.)* Can I touch it?

DOUG. Why.

KAYLEEN. Can I?

DOUG. Okay. *(Kayleen touches Doug's wound.)*

KAYLEEN. Gross.

DOUG. Your hands are cold.

KAYLEEN. It's because I wash them a lot. You should wash your hands. They are grimy.

DOUG. *(Showing his hands.)* I fell. There's pieces of rock in them. *(Kayleen kneels down and takes his hand and starts to pick pieces of gravel out of his palm. Doug stares at her, transfixed as she does this. Quietly.)* Ow.

KAYLEEN. Does it hurt?

DOUG. A little. *(Lights shift. Music fills and Kayleen and Doug prepare for Scene 2.)*

Scene 2

Age Twenty-Three: Eye Blown Out

Fifteen years later. The kids are 23.

A hospital room. Doug sits on an examining table. He's wearing a black suit spattered with blood. He has an enormous bandage across his face, covering specifically his left eye. He looks dazed. His front tooth is missing.

Kayleen enters. She wears a black dress and heels. She also looks dazed. She has mud all over her feet and lower legs.

She sees Doug like this for the first time.

They stare at each other.

DOUG. The fireworks were awesome.
KAYLEEN. Shut up. Okay? Just shut up, Doug. You shouldn't be left alone with explosives.
DOUG. I didn't want to be alone.
KAYLEEN. Oh, it's *my* fault? The night before I have to bury my father?
DOUG. What are you even doing here?
KAYLEEN. Kristen MacConnell called me.
DOUG. Kristen from high school?
KAYLEEN. She's a nurse here. She said you came in and you kept saying my name. So she called me. They thought you tried to kill yourself.
DOUG. Who tries to kill themself with a firework?
KAYLEEN. I know. I told them, no, you're just a crackhead dumbass with shit for brains. I told them you'd never commit suicide because you wouldn't have any scars to show off afterwards. Anyway, she said you got hurt.

DOUG. Why'd you come?

KAYLEEN. I don't know, Dougie. I was asleep on the kitchen table.

DOUG. What?

KAYLEEN. I had some drinks when I got home.

DOUG. What about that guy. That guy. That guy you live with.

KAYLEEN. He's sleeping. He was sleeping when I got home. His name is Brad.

DOUG. His name is ass-face. Why do you have mud all over your legs.

KAYLEEN. I drove halfway, but the car got stuck in the mud.

DOUG. What do you mean?

KAYLEEN. I mean, I drove part of the way until the car got stuck in the mud.

DOUG. The car got stuck in the mud.

KAYLEEN. Yeah.

DOUG. What are you even talking about? What mud? Where is there mud between the hospital and your house that you could get stuck in?

KAYLEEN. Just don't … Just shut up. There's mud. On the side of the road.

DOUG. What, you veered off the road? Are you drunk?

KAYLEEN. No! It's just the windshield is all jacked up because Brad hit a tree last February, and I couldn't see, and there was this mist or fog or something. And I drank a few vodkas. But I mostly slept those off.

DOUG. So you just left the car.

KAYLEEN. You know how I get.

DOUG. How you get?

KAYLEEN. Fuck you. You know how I get. When you get hurt. You know.

DOUG. *(Matter of fact.)* Doctor said I'm gonna be blind in one eye.

KAYLEEN. *(Quietly.)* Dougie … *(She sits near him, covers her eyes briefly with her hands.)*

DOUG. *(Not sad, just observing.)* It's gone. The whole thing. But I think it wasn't just the poke. It was the burn, too. The thing kept burning once it had punctured the eye. And so the burn really messed it all up.

KAYLEEN. You always had problems with that eye.

DOUG. Yeah.

KAYLEEN. The chopping wedge.

12

DOUG. The wedge.

KAYLEEN. And that girl who skated on your eye, right? When you were little? And then senior year. The Tabasco sauce.

DOUG. And pink eye.

KAYLEEN. Yeah.

DOUG. I gave you pink eye that time.

KAYLEEN. No, you didn't. I never got it.

DOUG. I think about that all the time. *(Beat.)* I think about that all the time. I always think about it.

KAYLEEN. Yeah, well, you're a freak.

DOUG. I didn't want you to come in here.

KAYLEEN. Yeah, right.

DOUG. I mean, I'm glad you're here. For sure. But you have the funeral tomorrow and everything. You should go home. Take a bath. Get some rest.

KAYLEEN. Shut up. I don't feel like walking back to my car just yet.

DOUG. Wow, you're really drunk, aren't you?

KAYLEEN. No, I'm just bleary. I feel like I just woke up. You don't understand the week I've had. I have to get a call at work to tell me my dad's lying dead in the driveway. And then dealing with everyone. And this shit. And then tonight, you come riding into town. Here's Dougie, five years later all of a sudden. I haven't slept. I just haven't slept in like … I don't know. Four years or something. *(Doug holds up four fingers.)*

DOUG. How many fingers am I holding up?

KAYLEEN. Four. *(Doug holds up his middle finger.)*

DOUG. How about now?

KAYLEEN. Shut up.

DOUG. We can both hardly see. *(Kayleen smiles at him.)*

KAYLEEN. Maybe that's for the best. *(Long silence.)*

DOUG. I think I'm seeing two of you.

KAYLEEN. I'm seeing two of you, too.

DOUG. Let's dance.

KAYLEEN. Shut up.

DOUG. No, we're both seeing double. We can dance, all four of us, we can play Ring Around the Rosie.

KAYLEEN. Sit down. *(Doug pulls her up.)* I'm seriously dizzy!

DOUG. Me too! *(They sway strangely with each other. Sings, any random melody.)*

    Ohhh Leenie …

Leenie Deenie …
Leenie Deenie Weenie Moe.
Moe Weenie.
My Leenie Deenie Diney Doo.
Diney doo.
Diney doo.
(They both dance and laugh. Doug takes her hand and puts it over his face.) Will you touch it?

KAYLEEN. What?

DOUG. My eye.

KAYLEEN. You don't have an eye.

DOUG. My eye socket.

KAYLEEN. That's disgusting. *(She stops dancing with him and leans against the bed.)* I probably can't smoke in here, right?

DOUG. Will you touch it?

KAYLEEN. What are you talking about. Stop being weird.

DOUG. You've always been able to mend my wounds.

KAYLEEN. Great. Glad I could've been of service. *(She takes out a pack of cigarettes.)* I'm just going to smoke. What are they going to do?

DOUG. I know it's probably superstition, but I kind of need it. You know you always do it.

KAYLEEN. I don't always do anything.

DOUG. You've got like super powers. Even tonight. When we kissed, you kissed my missing tooth. The gap. And it stopped hurting.

KAYLEEN. Well, I'm not touching your disgusting eye socket. *(Doug starts to pick at the bandages around his head.)* What are you doing?

DOUG. You'll do it. You'll touch it. You'll heal me. The pills only last so long.

KAYLEEN. Stop that.

DOUG. Once the pills wear off, it's going to kill again. You've got to just touch it.

KAYLEEN. Doug, stop doing that! *(Doug starts unpeeling the bandages around his face. He unpeels the top layer off, and then starts unwrapping another layer.)*

DOUG. It's okay. I know what I'm doing / okay?

KAYLEEN. / I really don't want to see / this!

DOUG. / I just need you to help me out, Leenie. You know. You know what you do. *(It's all off except for an extremely bloody gauze pad taped over his left eye. It looks ghoulish, disgusting, frightening.)* Will you please touch my / eye?

KAYLEEN. / Get away from me! Doug, I can't look at that! Please?! Put your … Put that stuff back over it! This can't be healthy, / come on!
DOUG. / You can make it better.
KAYLEEN. No, no I can't, leave me alone.
DOUG. Just touch it! Once!
KAYLEEN. *(With fury.)* NO! I WILL NOT! I'm not here to TAKE CARE OF YOU, Doug. I am not a *healer.*
DOUG. I'm in pain, do you understand that?!
KAYLEEN. I don't care!
DOUG. *Then leave! Get out of here, fucking go! (For an instant they are both startled. Then she exits. Lights shift. Music fills and Kayleen and Doug prepare for Scene 3.)*

Scene 3

Age Thirteen: The Limbo

Ten years earlier. The kids are 13.

The nurse's office. Night.

Kayleen enters. She is unwell. She wipes her mouth from having just coughed something up. She's unsteady. She is dressed for the 8th grade dance.

She lays on the bed, feet still on the floor.

Doug enters, hopping on one foot. He sits quickly in the other bed.

DOUG. *(In pain.)* Ah! Ah! Ah! *(Kayleen looks up at him.)*
KAYLEEN. What happened to you?
DOUG. I was rocking out.

KAYLEEN. You were dancing?

DOUG. Yeah. I was all over the place.

KAYLEEN. Were you "break" dancing?

DOUG. No, man. It was the limbo.

KAYLEEN. Did you hurt your ankle?

DOUG. Yeah. What's wrong with you?

KAYLEEN. Nothing.

DOUG. I mean: What about the dance?

KAYLEEN. What about it.

DOUG. It's going on!

KAYLEEN. Big deal.

DOUG. You don't like it?

KAYLEEN. No.

DOUG. It's fun.

KAYLEEN. So go back to it.

DOUG. I jacked up my ankle.

KAYLEEN. Doing the limbo.

DOUG. Yeah, it's Mexican, you know? I was rocking out. How come you don't like it.

KAYLEEN. I just don't.

DOUG. So why'd you come?

KAYLEEN. Shut up. *(Long beat.)*

DOUG. Did you throw up blood?

KAYLEEN. What?!

DOUG. I heard Sister Boniface tell Mrs. Wheaton that you had thrown up blood.

KAYLEEN. I didn't throw up blood. I just threw up.

DOUG. You want me to get you some ginger ale?

KAYLEEN. No. Thank you.

DOUG. I can throw up whenever I want.

KAYLEEN. That's reassuring.

DOUG. Really, though. I don't need to like stick my finger down my throat or anything. I can just do it, if I want.

KAYLEEN. Why would you want to.

DOUG. Sometimes, you know, just to feel better. Or, like to gross people out, or something. I was playing hockey? I play hockey. I was playing and this dude on the other team, he was a real agitator. And he kept creeping all over me, he was annoying you know? He was just annoying. And so I made myself throw up a little bit in my mouth? And I spat it on him.

16

KAYLEEN. That is the most disgusting thing I've ever heard in my life. You're disgusting.

DOUG. Man! He got so grossed out he started to cry. And then I was like, skating all over the place. I scored a goal. We lost, but I still scored a goal.

KAYLEEN. Hockey sounds like a wonderful activity.

DOUG. I tore my Achilles tendon last summer.

KAYLEEN. Why are you talking to me right now? Why don't you go back to your dance?

DOUG. But that's why I just hurt my ankle. It never really healed right, I think. Sometimes I hurt it just by walking. Do you know how I did it?

KAYLEEN. You said: Dancing.

DOUG. No, I mean tore my tendon.

KAYLEEN. I don't know. Playing hockey?

DOUG. Nope. Uh-uh. I was riding on the handlebars. Todd Scott was riding and I was on the handlebars and we were speeding down the Noble Road hill and my foot got caught in the spokes and I got flipped off the bike. I also got 10 stitches in my face. But also, I tore my Achilles tendon. I'm accident prone. That's what my mom says I am.

KAYLEEN. If you're riding on the handlebars of a bike going down a hill, you're not accident prone, you're retarded.

DOUG. You shouldn't say "retarded." That's real rude to retarded people.

KAYLEEN. Sorry I offended you.

DOUG. No, it's cool. *(The pulse of music can be heard echoing in the distance. Nodding his head with music.)* Aw yeah. I like this one. You wanna dance?

KAYLEEN. What are you talking about. *(Doug gets up, gimpy, but spirited. He starts to dance awkwardly.)*

DOUG. Let's dance!

KAYLEEN. Yeah, right.

DOUG. I'm serious! I wanna dance with you. Get it up!

KAYLEEN. I'm not dancing!

DOUG. Come on! *(Doug pulls her off the bed and they very awkwardly dance to the distant music. But it's too awkward and Kayleen walks away and flops on the bed.)* What?

KAYLEEN. So! Retarded!

DOUG. How come you don't like to dance?

KAYLEEN. Would you just leave me alone?

DOUG. Go up with me.

KAYLEEN. I'm not going back to the dance, okay? Leave me alone.

DOUG. But it's fun.

KAYLEEN. It's not fun for me. *(Doug stares at her for a moment. He sits, takes off his shoe, and starts scratching the bottom of his foot vigorously.)* What are you DOING?

DOUG. Got an itchy foot.

KAYLEEN. That's disgusting.

DOUG. So? So is throwing up blood.

KAYLEEN. I didn't throw up blood. *(Doug continues scratching his foot. Kayleen watches him, unguarded, for a moment. Then she turns away.)*

DOUG. So … Kaitlin … Who do you like?

KAYLEEN. What did you just call me?

DOUG. Kaitlin.

KAYLEEN. My name is Kayleen.

DOUG. Oh, yeah, Kayleen. I meant to say Kayleen.

KAYLEEN. You're a dick.

DOUG. I am not.

KAYLEEN. Shut up. *(Doug takes off his other shoe. He scratches that foot, but not nearly as vigorously.)*

DOUG. So who do you like?

KAYLEEN. *(Irritated.)* I don't understand the question.

DOUG. Which guy do you like?

KAYLEEN. I hate everybody.

DOUG. Why?

KAYLEEN. I just do. Shut up. *(Doug stops scratching his feet. He looks at them. Stretches. He takes off his socks.)*

DOUG. Hey Kayleen.

KAYLEEN. What.

DOUG. Look! *(Kayleen looks at him and he whips one of his socks at her face.)*

KAYLEEN. *(Totally skeeved.)* EW! EW! That's so gross!

DOUG. It's my sock!

KAYLEEN. I know!

DOUG. It's stanky! It's smelly!

KAYLEEN. That's the grossest thing I've ever seen! You are disgusting! Get away from me!

DOUG. WHO DO YOU LIKE?

KAYLEEN. Just go away!

DOUG. There's not one guy you like?

KAYLEEN. I told you, NO. Leave me alone. *(Doug goes and picks up his sock and takes it back to his bed.)* You're so stupid.

DOUG. I like Erin Marks.

KAYLEEN. Good for you.

DOUG. She's really pretty. I danced with her tonight. She kissed Dan Strauss.

KAYLEEN. Yeah, she also kissed Ian McGee.

DOUG. She did?

KAYLEEN. Yes. *(Doug thinks about this.)*

DOUG. She did not.

KAYLEEN. I saw them kissing backstage at the choir concert.

DOUG. Have you ever kissed anyone?

KAYLEEN. You are so stupid.

DOUG. I am not. Have you?

KAYLEEN. Shut up. *(Doug is quiet for a moment. He goes and gets his sock. He puts both socks back on.)*

DOUG. I haven't ever kissed anyone.

KAYLEEN. I don't care.

DOUG. I'm going to kiss Erin Marks tonight.

KAYLEEN. Good for you. *(Doug lies down on the bed. He stretches.)* Why don't you just go back up there?

DOUG. I'm gonna go in a second. *(Kayleen lies down. They both face the ceiling.)* I think kissing is going to be really nice.

KAYLEEN. You're retarded. *(Doug starts kissing his forearm and the crook of his arm, as if to practice. He gets more and more passionate, trying to annoy Kayleen.)*

DOUG. Mmm. Kiss. Kissy Kiss. Kissy Kiss Kiss. *(Kayleen gets up to leave.)*

KAYLEEN. I'm leaving. You are so annoying and stupid.

DOUG. I'm not stupid. That's really mean, you know? Everyone just thinks just because I'm awesome at sports and I always get hurt that I'm stupid, but I'm not stupid, I'm just brave, that's all. I'm brave. Don't leave.

KAYLEEN. I thought you wanted to go back to the dance.

DOUG. Not yet. I want to sit here. *(Kayleen goes back and sits down.)* I'm not always brave.

KAYLEEN. Yeah. I know. *(Beat.)*

DOUG. Do you want to practice kissing?

KAYLEEN. *WHAT?*

DOUG. I'm just saying: I never kissed anyone. And I'm assuming you haven't either. And I'm nervous about doing it, and you probably are too, so why don't we just practice so when we do have our first kiss, we'll know what we're doing.

KAYLEEN. No thank you.

DOUG. Come on.

KAYLEEN. No.

DOUG. Come on.

KAYLEEN. No, I'm not going to kiss you! That's gross! And besides, we wouldn't have a "first kiss" after that. That would BE our "first kiss." And I don't want my first kiss to be with you. And I just threw up anyhow.

DOUG. It wouldn't be our first kiss, it would be a practice kiss. I don't like you, I like Erin Marks.

KAYLEEN. I just threw up.

DOUG. Didn't you wash out your mouth?

KAYLEEN. Yeah.

DOUG. So that's okay then. Come on. *(He stands up.)* Kayleen, come on. Practice kiss. Then we go back up to the dance.

KAYLEEN. I can't even believe you're talking about this.

DOUG. Come on. Practice kiss.

KAYLEEN. This is just weird. Let's just go back to the dance. *(Kayleen gets up. Doug leans in. His face hovers just in front of hers. She looks at him, then allows Doug to kiss her. They kiss. Then they step apart. They look at each other for a moment. Kayleen puts her hand over her mouth.)*

DOUG. What's wrong? *(She's going to puke. She grabs a trash can and throws up in it. She throws up a lot. When she's done, she just stands there, holding the trash can.)* Are you okay? *(Kayleen won't look at him. She's clearly humiliated.)* Kayleen, you okay?

KAYLEEN. Just please go. *(Doug looks at her. She holds the trash can close to her body. Doug cocks his head back and makes a really strange sound, like a deep groan or gargle. He keeps doing this and then grabs the trash can from Kayleen and he throws up into it. When he's done. He shakes his head, as if to clear it. And he stares into the trash can.)*

DOUG. Our throw up is all mixed together. *(Looks at Kayleen.)* You wanna see? *(Kayleen stares at him, and then steps to him and she and Doug look in the trash can together.)* So awesome.

KAYLEEN. Yeah. Yeah. *(Lights shift. Music fills and Kayleen and Doug prepare for Scene 4.)*

Scene 4

Age Twenty-Eight: Tuesday

Fifteen years later. The kids are 28.

Hospital. Doug is in a coma. He wears an eyepatch over his left eye.

Kayleen enters. She hasn't seen him like this.

KAYLEEN. *(To herself.)* Goddamnit. *(She goes to Doug. Only beeping and other artificial sounds. She looks at him for a long time.)* Hey again. *(Kayleen covers her face with her hands and then she exits. She reenters quickly.)* So I'm trying to get more healthy. Mostly. Most of the time. I thought you should know. So, you know, don't worry about me or anything. *(A long moment.)* Come on, Doug. Wake up now. Just wake up. I'm here. I'm here to wake you up, okay? It's been a long time, I know, and I just want to … *(Kayleen shakes her head, realizing she's basically talking to herself.)* Jesus. What the fuck am I doing here? *(She goes into her bag and gets some pills. She takes them. She sits down in a chair that's not close to the bed.)* I'm so sick of your shit. *(Kayleen rubs her temples. She gets up and walks to him quickly.)* WHO GETS STRUCK BY FUCKING LIGHTNING?! *(She goes back to her seat and collapses in it.)* ON THEIR FUCKING ROOF! I hate to tell you this, you stupid fucking genius, but getting up on the roof in the middle of a fucking electrical storm isn't a brilliant fucking move! *(Kayleen calms herself. She takes out a bottle of lotion and takes some in her hands.)* I'm trying not to swear so much. And I'm moisturizing. So that's what's going on with me these days. *(She rubs lotion into her hands.)* So congratulations on almost being married. I mean, I heard about it. I heard about her. *Elaine. Elaine.* She sounds lovely. Poor girl. You probably made the right decision, though. I don't think you're gonna be ready to settle down till you stop climbing up on the roof, you know? I mean, I'm no model citizen, but I do know basic fucking things about personal safety, you dumb piece of shit. *(Kayleen puts her lotion back in her bag. She gets up and walks over to Doug again.)* I mean, you're not the first groom to get cold feet. *(Kayleen shakes her head and wanders around the room.)* I feel like an idiot here. I was pretty sure, I'd get here, say two words to you and you'd snap out of this shit. Because it's ME! It's KAYLEEN, DOUGIE! I'm BACK! Last time I saw you you'd just blown out your stupid eye. It was this same hospital. *(She goes back to her chair.)* Twice in ten years. Not stellar for a couple of kids supposed to be best friends. Twice! Well, I guess this is three times. Does this count? Does it count if one of us might be brain dead? Of course, you've always been brain dead, haven't you, Dougie? Ha ha ha. *(Kayleen rubs her face.)* What else what else what else what else…? *(Kayleen gets up and looks at Doug. She slowly walks to him and touches his hand. She takes his hand in hers. This is the first time in this scene she's really let herself look at him. She gingerly holds out her hands over him, as if she had the power to raise the dead but knows she looks ridiculous. She touches his chest and then lifts her hands up, as if she might have just woken him. Nothing.)* I am retarded. *(She walks in a circle, and then comes back to him. She stares at him for a long moment. She holds his hand, rubs it. She goes to her bag, gets out the lotion, comes back to him.)* Your hand is all dry. *(She moisturizes his hand.)* You can't marry that girl, Doug. You can't. Because what about me? What about me, huh? When my dad died, when you … when you came to the funeral home that night … That stuff you said to me … You're always doing that, you know? The top ten best things anyone's ever done for me have all been done by you. That's pretty good, right? And I know. I know I know I know … I'm so stupid. I'm always … I'm just fucked up, you know that. And so I need you to stick it out, Dougie. I'm gonna need you to come looking for me again. I'm sorry. But you have to wake up now. You have to wake up for me. Because I'm *not* great, you know? I'm not great. And I really need you right now. I really need you to come over and show me some stupid shit again, tell me some stupid joke like you always do. I'm sorry I've been gone. I'm back now. You know? I'm back now. So wake up. Wake up now, buddy. Just, you know … rise and shine. It's Tuesday. That was always your favorite day. *(Lights shift. Music fills and Kayleen and Doug prepare for Scene 5.)*

Scene 5

Age Eighteen: Pink Eye

Ten years earlier. The kids are 18.

Kayleen's bedroom. Kayleen sits on her bed, knees to her chest. Doug enters. He's beaten up pretty badly. He carries an enormous hockey duffel bag. He's in pain. He drops the bag, collapses against her bed, and yells in pain.

KAYLEEN. What are you *doing*?
DOUG. Had to stop by.
KAYLEEN. What *happened*?
DOUG. Matty Dozier happened.
KAYLEEN. What do you mean?
DOUG. I got in a fight with him.
KAYLEEN. *(Very concerned.)* You got in a fight with MATTY DOZIER?
DOUG. Yeah. And then that stupid Girl Scout gave me pink eye. *(He takes Girl Scout cookies out of his bag and throws them at Kayleen.)* Here. I bought her stupid cookies. *Girl Scouts.* What a bunch of little bitches.
KAYLEEN. These are Samoas.
DOUG. Damn right.
KAYLEEN. Where are the Thin Mints?
DOUG. Fuck that.
KAYLEEN. Fuck you.
DOUG. What's *your* problem?
KAYLEEN. Go home. I'm sick. And you're annoying. I wanted Thin Mints.
DOUG. Shut up or I'll give you pink eye.
KAYLEEN. Go away. *(Doug gets up, starts rubbing his eyes. And then walks to her like Frankenstein.)*
DOUG. Give ... pink eye ... mmmmmh ...

KAYLEEN. Ew! Stop! Get away! *(Doug crawls all over her on the bed. Kayleen fights him off.)* Get OFF ME, you pervert!
DOUG. PINK EYE!!!
KAYLEEN. *(Very serious.)* GET OFF! GOD!
DOUG. What? What's wrong with you?
KAYLEEN. You're a fucking pervert! Every guy in the world! You all act like you're playing around, except you have to crawl all over me! You think I don't know you have a total hard-on right now, you perv!
DOUG. I do not!
KAYLEEN. You do too!
DOUG. I'm wearing a cup! *(Doug knocks on his crotch. It's plastic.)* It's a protective cup, you paranoid little horn dog.
KAYLEEN. Just leave me alone.
DOUG. Fine. *(Doug sits down and opens cookies. He eats.)* Ho bag.
KAYLEEN. Shut up.
DOUG. Enjoy the pink eye. It's like the most contagious thing in the entire world.
KAYLEEN. I don't care.
DOUG. What's wrong with you, anyway.
KAYLEEN. Nothing. I just am tired. What happened with Dozier.
DOUG. First, I punched him in the face.
KAYLEEN. Why? *(Doug shrugs.)* It's MATTY DOZIER, Dougie. You don't go punching Matty Dozier in the face. What do you have, a death wish?
DOUG. He threw me down and kicked me and wailed all over me. But I didn't care 'cause I busted his stupid nose. Fuckin' pussy. How come you weren't at school? Are you sick again?
KAYLEEN. I'm always sick.
DOUG. You don't look sick.
KAYLEEN. I'm not. Not right this minute, anyhow.
DOUG. But you sure look weird. And you're all rude and everything.
KAYLEEN. Probably 'cause I totally had sex today. *(Doug chokes on his cookie.)*
DOUG. What?
KAYLEEN. With Tim.
DOUG. You had … TODAY!? WHEN? How? What are you TALKING ABOUT?
KAYLEEN. He's my boyfriend.
DOUG. So? I know!
KAYLEEN. So we have sex!

DOUG. You mean … you've been HAVING sex? How long?!

KAYLEEN. Like two weeks. We did it two weeks ago.

DOUG. How come you didn't tell me?

KAYLEEN. I'm telling you now!

DOUG. Well what the fuck?!

KAYLEEN. WHAT?

DOUG. I don't want you having sex with TIM!

KAYLEEN. He's my boyfriend!

DOUG. You're too young!

KAYLEEN. Just because you've never had sex.

DOUG. I told you I did have sex.

KAYLEEN. With your cousin.

DOUG. *We're not cousins, we're family friends!* Shut up! I can't believe you had sex with TIM. That guy is nasty.

KAYLEEN. It's not like we've been doing it non-stop anyway. We only had sex twice.

DOUG. Twice?

KAYLEEN. Once two weeks ago. And then today.

DOUG. TODAY? Here?! In this bed? EWW! I was just in this bed that you were screwing Tim Reilly in? That guy is skeeze central.

KAYLEEN. Just forget about it then.

DOUG. I can't just forget about it!

KAYLEEN. It wasn't …

DOUG. … What?

KAYLEEN. Nothing.

DOUG. *What?*

KAYLEEN. Nothing. I just. It's over anyway. I mean. I did it. Twice. I got that over with.

DOUG. Sounds like it was really fun.

KAYLEEN. It wasn't, okay? It wasn't fun. It was … It was just like, you know. Like you have to pretend you're not even doing anything, like you're just playing around, like you were with me, just now. Tim's over here, and we have to pretend like we're just being normal, you know, playing around, wrestling around and everything and then suddenly we're not, suddenly he's like … you know …

DOUG. He's like what?

KAYLEEN. Nothing.

DOUG. You didn't WANT to?

KAYLEEN. I mean … not at that exact moment … *(Doug stands up, stares at her.)*

25

DOUG. Kayleen …

KAYLEEN. Don't get all crazy. You're always so dramatic.

DOUG. I'm going to fucking kill him

KAYLEEN. No you're not.

DOUG. I'm gonna kick him in his ugly skull, that dirty piece of shit.

KAYLEEN. You're not going to do that.

DOUG. Why not?

KAYLEEN. Because you're not, okay? Just forget about it!

DOUG. *(Starting to lose it.)* I'm talking about you, Kayleen! I'm talking about you, and nobody can just come around and … I'm gonna kill him. I'm gonna kill him. I'm gonna fucking / kill him … I'm gonna kill him …

KAYLEEN. / Will you shut up PLEASE? Will you just sit here?

DOUG. NO I'M NOT GOING TO SIT DOWN!

KAYLEEN. He's my boyfriend!

DOUG. No he's not! Not anymore! I hate him I hate him I hate him so much … *(Doug puts his face in his hands.)*

KAYLEEN. Doug … Doug, come on. Are you crying?

DOUG. *(Not removing his hands; crying.)* NO. *(Kayleen grabs his shirt and pulls him to the bed where he sits, still face in hands. Kayleen hugs him. Doug wipes his eyes.)* Why's everyone got to be so mean? Dozier … Tim … they don't … They're all such … *(Beat.)* He called you a skank. Dozier did. I was leaving school and he yelled out to me and … him and all those guys were laughing and just … saying all this stuff and … People think they can say things like that about you, but then they get punched in the face, and they always will, Kayleen, they will always get punched in the face. By me. *(Beat.)* You're not a skank. You're not. *(They sit for a moment. He looks at her and then at her hands. He strokes her leg in a tender way.)* You got blood on your jeans.

KAYLEEN. It's not blood.

DOUG. Yeah it is. Yeah it is. *(He looks at her.)* When you start that again?

KAYLEEN. I didn't start anything. *(Doug looks at her. She looks away.)* I thought having sex would, you know. I thought it might make me stop.

DOUG. Does it hurt?

KAYLEEN. A little.

DOUG. What could make you stop?

26

KAYLEEN. I don't know. Nothing. *(Doug gets up and walks away from her. Kayleen watches him. She unbuttons her jeans and pulls them down. Her thighs have small cuts on them.)* Look. *(Doug looks at her legs. He goes to her. He kneels in front of her and lightly touches them.)*

DOUG. You think I could give your legs pink eye?

KAYLEEN. Maybe.

DOUG. Yeah. Maybe. *(Doug studies her legs.)* What do you use? *(Kayleen takes a razor blade from underneath her pillow.)* If it hurts, why do you do it?

KAYLEEN. I don't know. *(Doug touches her legs gently. They look at each other.)* Don't tell me to stop. *(Doug stands up and unbuttons his pants. He pulls them down. He holds his thigh out to her.)* I'm not going to cut you.

DOUG. I won't tell you to stop if you do.

KAYLEEN. Why.

DOUG. Just do it. Just like how you do it. *(Kayleen puts the razor to his thigh, but doesn't cut him.)*

KAYLEEN. I can't.

DOUG. Do it.

KAYLEEN. Dougie, why?

DOUG. Just do it. I want to see what it's like, okay?

KAYLEEN. It's different. I can't do it to someone else.

DOUG. I'm not someone else. I'm you. *(She looks at him. She puts the razor to his thigh. She cuts him. He breaths sharply, once.)*

KAYLEEN. I'm sorry … *(He touches his cut. He kneels back down in front of her. He puts his hands on her thighs. She puts her hands on top of his hands. They look at each other.)*

DOUG. You're the prettiest girl I've ever seen.

KAYLEEN. I know. *(Lights shift. Music fills and Kayleen and Doug prepare for Scene 6.)*

Scene 6

Age Thirty-Three: A Blue Raspberry Dip

Fifteen years later. The kids are 33.

A sterile lounge in a health facility. Kayleen sits in a chair, staring into space. Doug enters. He walks with a cane and a pronounced limp. He wears an eyepatch. He sees her before she sees him.

DOUG. Leenie. *(She doesn't notice. Louder.)* Kayleen. *(She turns to see him.)*
KAYLEEN. I thought you were dead.
DOUG. I wasn't.
KAYLEEN. You woke up.
DOUG. Yeah.
KAYLEEN. When?
DOUG. Five years ago.
KAYLEEN. Five years?
DOUG. Yeah.
KAYLEEN. You really woke up five years ago? Where have you been?
DOUG. I don't know. *(Beat.)*
KAYLEEN. What's with the cane?
DOUG. Nothing.
KAYLEEN. Come on, what happened? *(Doug shrugs.)* Did you ever marry that girl?
DOUG. Elaine?
KAYLEEN. *Elaine.*
DOUG. You heard about that?
KAYLEEN. Yeah.
DOUG. No.
KAYLEEN. I thought you were dead.
DOUG. Did you visit me?
KAYLEEN. They've got me on about twenty-five medications or

28

something. Like a swirl of ice cream in me. You know how they dip the ice cream and it gets a hardened shell?

DOUG. Like at the Frostee Freeze.

KAYLEEN. I'm a blue raspberry dip.

DOUG. Delicious.

KAYLEEN. Yeah. *(Beat.)* This place isn't too bad. Except for the food and you can't smoke. *(Beat.)* I had a bad patch, Dougie.

DOUG. What did you do?

KAYLEEN. I hurt myself.

DOUG. How.

KAYLEEN. I don't remember doing it.

DOUG. Doing what?

KAYLEEN. My stomach. You know, it always hurt. And my mom, and all that. And it got worse, and I just tried to take it out.

DOUG. What do you mean.

KAYLEEN. I was out of my head. I tried to cut my stomach out. *(Beat. Doug flinches.)*

DOUG. That sort of thing. It's not healthy.

KAYLEEN. It was okay. I'm not very good with a knife.

DOUG. Kayleen … You visited me, didn't you? In the hospital? Because I swear to God I heard your voice out there. Or your presence or, what, your echo … I don't know how, but I remember you, something about you … coming to me, and sinking into me, and giving me breath again. You came and healed me.

KAYLEEN. What does it matter?

DOUG. What do you mean what does it matter? You raised me from the dead!

KAYLEEN. No, I DID NOT! I'm not your guardian fucking angel, Doug, for God's sake look at me, okay? I didn't come and see you.

DOUG. No. No no no, you can't lie to me. I can see it all over your face, you were there. You were *there.*

KAYLEEN. *(With rage.) I wasn't fucking there!*

DOUG. *(Angry; slams cane.)* Well, why NOT?

KAYLEEN. Because why would I, Doug? What about when *I* needed somebody?! Where were *you* the last five years?

DOUG. My life got away from me.

KAYLEEN. Poor you.

DOUG. Every angle of it. I probably have ten thousand excuses, but I … Kayleen, I'm sorry. Something happened to me and I had to find you. Look … *(Doug goes into his bag and takes out a small stone statue of an owl.)* I brought you this.

KAYLEEN. What is it?

DOUG. You don't remember?

KAYLEEN. No.

DOUG. You don't remember this owl.

KAYLEEN. *No.*

DOUG. Yes you do.

KAYLEEN. Am I supposed to?

DOUG. Stop LYING!

KAYLEEN. I'm NOT!

DOUG. You know this owl! We used to think it was an angel, back at school! It was a small statue on the roof of Saint Margaret Mary's.

KAYLEEN. I don't remember.

DOUG. You're full of SHIT!

KAYLEEN. I don't remember anything, okay? I'm sorry! How'd you get it?

DOUG. St. Margaret Mary's blew up.

KAYLEEN. *What?*

DOUG. It exploded.

KAYLEEN. Were there kids in it?

DOUG. No, you idiot. It closed down like ten years ago. It was used by the diocese for storage. There was a leaking gas main. Kaboom.

KAYLEEN. So what, you went to pick through the rubble?

DOUG. No, I work in insurance now.

KAYLEEN. *What.*

DOUG. I'm a claims adjuster.

KAYLEEN. You're such a loser.

DOUG. I know. But I got to go and investigate the wreckage. I go over and the place is collapsed. So I hoist myself up there and I'm walking on the roof and then I stepped through a weak board or something and this upright nail went clear through my foot. It was about eight inches long. Then the board with the nail in it — *that* board snapped through another board and I broke my leg in three places. It took them five hours to get me out. And then I got an infection. And that's why I have this cane now. But listen: I'm up there, you know? Stuck up there, waiting for them to come and get me. And there were these severed heads of a bunch of saints that had ended up all over the place, and they were just staring at me. And this owl was there too. And so I lean over and grab the little guy. I was in some serious pain, you know? And I just gripped him close to me, because … Because all of a sudden, I was like, *Where the fuck is Kayleen?* You know? All of a sudden, everything was clear … trapped up on that roof, impaled, surrounded by all the angels and saints … That's my life, up there, Leenie. That's my life without you. *(Beat.)*

KAYLEEN. Does it hurt?

DOUG. It's Stigmata!

KAYLEEN. It's not Stigmata, it's one foot. Stigmata is both feet and both hands. Let's keep perspective.

DOUG. It hurts a little. *(Long beat. Kayleen holds the owl and looks at him.)*

KAYLEEN. Look at this poor guy. He's all beat up.

DOUG. Spent his whole life up there on that roof. Looking down. *(Beat.)*

KAYLEEN. Do you want to touch my scar? *(Doug doesn't answer. They stare at each other for a moment. She gets up and goes to him. She pulls her shirt out so Doug can put his hand up her shirt. He does and touches her stomach.)*

DOUG. God, Leenie.

KAYLEEN. That's my scar, Dougie. It's like a roller coaster across my stomach. You're not the only retardo on the planet. *(She tenderly touches his head. He takes her face in his hands. His hand remains up her shirt.)* You didn't even like him. You said he was a stupid-looking angel.

DOUG. You do remember.

KAYLEEN. Yes, goddamnit, I remember my goddamn angel. *(They sway together for a moment.)*

DOUG. I wish I could do to you what you do to me. *(Beat.)* I wish you'd let me. *(Beat.)* You think we could get out of here? You think we could just pry ourselves out of everything? Go somewhere else?

KAYLEEN. Somewhere else.

DOUG. Yeah. Anywhere.

KAYLEEN. I can't.

DOUG. Not even right this minute. Sometime soon, I could come and get you and …

KAYLEEN. I can't. I can't. *(Kayleen steps away from him. She stops looking at him. She sits back down, holding the owl. He stares at her. A long beat.)*

DOUG. Are you going let me drift away here? Because I don't want to, Leens. I'm worn out. I don't have so much left in me anymore you know? I'm saying, don't let me. Don't let me drift away again. I might not make it back. *(The lights shift. Music fills and Kayleen and Doug prepare for Scene 7.)*

Scene 7

Age Twenty-Three: Tooth and Nail

Ten years earlier. The kids are 23.

Night, outside of a funeral home. Kayleen sits on the steps of the funeral home, smoking. She wears the same black dress from Scene 2, but she looks clean and sober.

Doug enters. He's wearing the black suit from Scene 2, but no blood, and he still has his left eye. He's missing one of his front teeth.

They look at each other.

DOUG. *(Smiles.)* Hey again.
KAYLEEN. What happened to your tooth?
DOUG. Knocked it out. This morning. I was hammering in the shed. Hi, Kayleen.
KAYLEEN. Hey again.
DOUG. I'm sorry.
KAYLEEN. For what.
DOUG. For your dad.
KAYLEEN. You're sorry for him.
DOUG. *About* him.

KAYLEEN. You missed the wake. Everyone went home. No one in there but a dead guy in a box.

DOUG. I thought it went till nine.

KAYLEEN. Eight-thirty.

DOUG. It's good to see you.

KAYLEEN. Fuck off. Toothless piece of shit. *(They smile at each other. Doug goes to her for a hug.)*

DOUG. It's so good to see you.

KAYLEEN. No, don't hug me. I'm all hugged out. I've been hugging people all day. Everyone in here: *I'm sorry for your loss. I'm so sorry for your loss.* What loss? If I hug one more person I'm going to choke on my own spit.

DOUG. It's been forever, Leenie.

KAYLEEN. I've been here. Where the fuck have you been?

DOUG. College.

KAYLEEN. College.

DOUG. I came back in the summers and Christmas. I tried to find you. I tried to look you up, but I couldn't find you.

KAYLEEN. I was here.

DOUG. Where? Not listed. Not at home.

KAYLEEN. I work. I work and I sleep. What do you do?

DOUG. Nothing. Not right now. Looking. I don't know. Seems whenever I'm home I'm looking for you.

KAYLEEN. You didn't look hard enough. *(Doug shakes himself out, as if waking from a dream or a trance.)*

DOUG. Jeez, Leenie, you're here now! I found you! *(He sits next to her and hugs her. She's annoyed.)*

KAYLEEN. Would you stop? You're a freak.

DOUG. I missed you. I missed you, Leenie.

KAYLEEN. Don't call me that. Nobody calls me that.

DOUG. I call you that. *(Beat.)* So what's been going on with you for the last four years? *(She moves away from him.)*

KAYLEEN. No, let's not do that. I don't feel like recapping the last four years of my life.

DOUG. Fine. *(Beat.)*

KAYLEEN. I'm waiting tables.

DOUG. Your dad told me you were waitressing. *(She looks at him, not expecting this.)* I told you, I came looking for you.

KAYLEEN. You talked to my dad?

DOUG. I came by your place.

KAYLEEN. When?

DOUG. This was like a year ago. I stopped to see if you were there. I talked to your dad. He told me you were waitressing but he didn't know where.

KAYLEEN. You *talked* to my dad?

DOUG. You think I enjoyed that? I hated being in the same room with that guy. May he rest in peace. *(Beat.)*

KAYLEEN. He never told me you stopped by.

DOUG. Big surprise there.

KAYLEEN. He's such an asshole. *(Beat.)* I'm alone now, Dougie.

DOUG. You're not alone.

KAYLEEN. Yeah, I am. My mom died last year.

DOUG. What? She died? When? How?

KAYLEEN. I don't know. Her stomach.

DOUG. Jesus, Leenie, I'm sorry.

KAYLEEN. Yeah, I know, you're *sorry for my loss* … I hadn't seen her in eleven years. Her ex-boyfriend called me to give me the news. You know what my dad said when I told him?

DOUG. What?

KAYLEEN. He started crying and told me she was a better woman than I'd ever be. This bitch who walked out on us. *(Beat.)*

DOUG. You're not alone, Leenie.

KAYLEEN. Don't call me that.

DOUG. *Leenie.*

KAYLEEN. Shut up.

DOUG. *Leenie Deenie.*

KAYLEEN. I'm going to burn you with my cigarette. *(He grins at her.)* You need to get a fake tooth, like, *stat.* You look inbred. *(Beat.)* Did it hurt?

DOUG. It hurt like crazy. *(Beat.)*

KAYLEEN. It's good to see you, too.

DOUG. I think I'm home now.

KAYLEEN. What's that mean?

DOUG. It means I'm home. I'm back.

KAYLEEN. Well, that's good, I guess.

DOUG. You know, whenever anything crazy happened in college, or I saw something amazing or beautiful or fucked up, I'd think, man, Leenie'd love this shit. Sometimes I'd just imagine you were there, you know, I'd imagine you were there and I'd start having a conversation with you. Just start talking to you.

KAYLEEN. Yeah, there's a word for that and it's SCHIZOPHRENIA.

DOUG. I just want to be friends again.

KAYLEEN. You're the one who left.

DOUG. Are you okay?

KAYLEEN. I'm fine.

DOUG. Are you okay?

KAYLEEN. I told you, I'm fine.

DOUG. Come here.

KAYLEEN. No.

DOUG. Kayleen, come here.

KAYLEEN. Fuck off. *(Doug walks to her. He takes her face in his hands. She tries to resist, but relents.)*

DOUG. Look at me.

KAYLEEN. *WHAT*, Doug. *(They stare at each other. He kisses her. She lets him, but doesn't kiss him back.)*

DOUG. I love you. *(She pulls away from him.)*

KAYLEEN. Your parents were here tonight.

DOUG. I know.

KAYLEEN. They sent flowers. Your mother said she was going to bring by a casserole. That's what your mom is like. She's the kind of woman who brings over a casserole.

DOUG. They love you, too.

KAYLEEN. This is so fucked up what you're doing right now.

DOUG. What are you / talking about…?

KAYLEEN. / Kissing me. Coming back like this. Telling me you love me, your parents love me. Just leave me alone.

DOUG. Leenie …

KAYLEEN. You're so stupid. You always think everything is one way, but you don't know anything.

DOUG. What?! What don't I know?

KAYLEEN. You don't know *me*, okay? You think I'm someone, some girl you dreamt up a million years ago.

DOUG. Well, then, who are you?

KAYLEEN. Nothing. Just shut up.

DOUG. No, who are you? Since I don't know anything, who are you?

KAYLEEN. Shut up. *(Doug goes to her and tries to kiss her, but she steps away and doesn't let him.)* Don't.

DOUG. Why not. *(She doesn't answer. She lights a cigarette.)* I've got some fireworks in my car.

KAYLEEN. You're retarded.

DOUG. I do. I've got a mess of them in my trunk. Killer, too. The Japanese shit.

KAYLEEN. We're not going to light off fireworks.

DOUG. Why not?

KAYLEEN. I don't know, Dougie. Maybe because we're not fifteen anymore? Or because you're retarded? Or because I have to wake up tomorrow for my father's funeral?

DOUG. We'll go to the bridge down on Roanoke. Just like old times.

KAYLEEN. I'm living with someone.

DOUG. You're living with someone ... what, like you have a roommate?

KAYLEEN. I'm living with a guy. We've been together for a year.

DOUG. Where is he? He's not with you?

KAYLEEN. He doesn't like funerals.

DOUG. He doesn't like funerals? This isn't a funeral. This is a wake.

KAYLEEN. He said seeing a dead body would wig him out. *(Beat.)* Just shut up.

DOUG. And you're WITH this guy.

KAYLEEN. Don't judge him. He's sensitive.

DOUG. Fuck him. Fuck him fuck him fuck him.

KAYLEEN. That's nice. *(Doug paces. He starts to leave. He comes back.)*

DOUG. You know what, Kayleen? Jesus Christ, you know, I came to your house last year and your dad was there, and I know he hates my guts, he always has, and he's like, *She is where she is. I don't know where the girl is.* He said he didn't care and didn't care to know. And I was about to just leave, but I didn't. I didn't and I said to that son of a bitch ... *(He turns to the funeral home and shouts at it.)* You remember, asshole? You dead piece of shit?! You remember what I said to you?! I said to him, you are fucking WORTHLESS. You have a daughter and she is a gift from God. She is the most perfect being to ever walk this earth and you don't even know it. And she loves you because you're her stupid father. But you've never loved her back, you've just damaged her and fucked her up, and never even bothered to notice she's this ANGEL. So FUCK YOU COCKSUCKER. *(Beat.)* And then I told him I hoped he'd die alone. Which he did. So I feel a little guilty about that now. *(Beat.)* I can take care of you, Leenie. *(Beat. He approaches her. She hasn't been looking at him, but she has been moved by his words. He reaches out and touches her face. She flinches, recoils from his touch, and steps away from him.)*

KAYLEEN. I don't need anyone to take care of me. *(Doug turns to leave.)* Where are you going.
DOUG. I'm going to go light up my fireworks. *(He exits.)*
KAYLEEN. Bye. *(She takes out a cigarette. Lights it. Looks out after him. Sits down. More to herself.)* Don't blow your face off. *(Lights shift. Music fills and Kayleen and Doug prepare for Scene 8.)*

Scene 8

Age Thirty-Eight: Zamboni

Fifteen years later.

The kids are 38.

An empty indoor ice rink. Kayleen stands on the ice.

After a moment, Doug enters. He is in a wheelchair. He wears a coat and a knit cap, and of course an eye patch. They haven't seen each other since he visited her in the hospital, five years ago. They look at each other but don't say anything. They both look out at the rink.

DOUG. I did a good job with that ice.
KAYLEEN. It looks like glass.
DOUG. They rebuilt the Zam for me. I can drive it with my hands. *(Beat.)* Last cut of the day. It's late.
KAYLEEN. I didn't know. About you. About the accident. *(Doug doesn't answer.)* After I got out … I was too …
DOUG. It's okay. I know.
KAYLEEN. It's cold.
DOUG. Ice rink. *(Beat.)* I watch the kids play hockey. Oh, they fly around. They fly around the rink. *(Beat.)* I like it at night after the last cut. Look at the ice, Kayleen.
KAYLEEN. Your mom told me I could find you here. She's so nice

to me. As if she doesn't know anything. Or maybe as if she knows everything. You and your family, Dougie. Nicest people in the world. And you have to get tangled up in the spokes of my train wreck.

DOUG. Trains don't have spokes. *(Beat.)*

KAYLEEN. Dougie ... Why do you do this? *(He doesn't answer.)* Where'd you learn how to climb a telephone pole?

DOUG. Easy to climb up. Not so easy to climb down. Especially in the pouring rain.

KAYLEEN. Why did you climb it?

DOUG. You were unlisted.

KAYLEEN. You're stupid.

DOUG. Maybe.

KAYLEEN. Not maybe.

DOUG. Maybe if I could climb to the top of this telephone pole in the rain at night, like the mast of a ship lost at sea, maybe I'll see the shine of you, bringing me home again. *(Beat.)* That's the maybe.

KAYLEEN. *(Quiet.)* That's stupid. *(Beat.)*

DOUG. Yeah, that's stupid. *(She looks at him, he looks at the ice. A long moment.)*

KAYLEEN. I came here to lay my hands on you, Dougie. I've never believed it, but I have to do it ... because if you believe it, that must be enough. *(Doug doesn't answer, doesn't look at her.)* I came and saw you when you were in the coma.

DOUG. You said you didn't.

KAYLEEN. I did. I came and saw you. I touched you. I felt like an idiot, but I did. And nothing happened, so I just felt it was stupid. But you woke up. You woke up, you freak.

DOUG. How come you said you didn't come see me.

KAYLEEN. I don't know, Doug, there you were, asking me if I was the reason you miraculously sprung back to life, I can't be the reason you're alive. Why would I be able to do something like that? *How* could I? I don't know what this stupid thing is anyway ... It's just ... Is it something that comes true if one person believes it? Or two people? If it is, I believe it. I'll believe anything, Dougie, I don't care. I'm ... *(Beat.)* I'm going to touch you now. Tell me where. Tell me where.

DOUG. Don't touch me. Kayleen.

KAYLEEN. I know. But ... I just think ...

DOUG. Don't touch me.

KAYLEEN. I want to, Dougie. I have to, you have to let me ...

DOUG. Do not touch me.

KAYLEEN. Not even for that, Dougie. For me. Just for me. Just for me.

DOUG. *(Almost desperate; as in "Please don't touch me.")* Please. *(Kayleen stands and goes back to the bench and sits. She covers her face with her hands for a moment.)* I'm good like this. I'm good. Don't need anything else. Except maybe when I see those kids flying around on the ice. But I'm done flying around. *(Beat.)*

KAYLEEN. God, I feel sick.

DOUG. Throw up.

KAYLEEN. I want to. *(Beat.)* Remember...?

DOUG. Yeah.

KAYLEEN. We stood there staring at it.

DOUG. Disgusting.

KAYLEEN. You cleaned it out.

DOUG. I did?

KAYLEEN. Yeah, you washed it out. We left. We went out to the playground.

DOUG. We sat on the swings.

KAYLEEN. We sat on the swings. You kept climbing up the swing chains and swinging from the top bar, like ten feet off the ground. And I told you you were stupid and going to crack open your head. So you came back down. And we sat on the swings.

DOUG. What did we talk about.

KAYLEEN. God, I don't know ... We talked about everything. We talked so long, it was the latest I'd ever stayed up in my life. It was almost morning when we left the swings. It was cold, and you gave me your jacket to wear. The playground was so pretty just then. The sky was starting to be blue. *(They look at the ice.)*

End of Play

PROPERTY LIST

Bandage and bloody gauze
Mud
Pack of cigarettes
Eyepatch
Handbag with pills, bottle of lotion
Big hockey duffel bag with Girl Scout cookies (Samoas)
Razor blade, pillow
Cane
Stone owl
Coat, knit cap
Wheelchair

SOUND EFFECTS

Music fill
Music from school dance, off
Beeping and hospital room sounds